Brent Darnell

International

THE TAO OF EMOTIONAL INTELLIGENCE

82 Ways to Improve Your Social Competence

Updated for EQi 2.0

By
G. Brent Darnell

Other books by G. Brent Darnell

The People Profit Connection, How Emotional Intelligence Can Maximize People Skills and Maximize Your Profits

Communication and Presentation Skills for Tough Guys

Relationship Skills for Tough Guys: 12 Steps to Great Relationships

Stress Management, Time Management, and Life Balance for Tough Guys: Creating Success on Your Terms

The Tough Guy Survival Kit: Includes all of the Tough Guy books

The Primal Safety Coloring Book

Big Mama's Country Cookbook: Recipes from the True South

Other resources by G. Brent Darnell

www.change-u.com
App: Tao of Emotional Intelligence available for Apple and Android

---

Cover design and layout by **Tudor Maier**

Credit: The I Ching Book of Changes, the Richard Wilhelm translation translated into English by Cary F. Baynes, Bollinger Series XIX. Copyright 1950, 1967 © renewed 1977 by Princeton University Press. Reprinted with permission.

This book is dedicated to my wife, **Andrea,**
who has the heart of a warrior.

Notes from the Author:

I am a speaker, teacher, and coach. I teach people skills to technical people using emotional intelligence as a foundation. Emotional intelligence can be defined as social competence, or the ability to deal with people. I am always looking for ways to teach the concept of emotional intelligence and the sixteen emotional competencies that we measure when we work with individuals on their personal development.

When I came across the I Ching (pronounced Yee Jing), an ancient Chinese book of wisdom, many years ago, I saw the parallels to emotional intelligence right away. The I Ching, or book of changes, is based on the Taoist concepts of the universe. Ancient Chinese sages laid down principles that if followed, will bring to the superior person good fortune, happiness, wisdom, and success. I have taken sixteen fundamental emotional competencies as measured by the EQi 2.0 emotional intelligence evaluation and cross referenced them to the I Ching.

By learning more about these emotional competencies, and more importantly, applying the principles from the I Ching, students will be able to master themselves. And as Lao Tzu said, "Mastering others is strength. Mastering yourself makes you fearless." Read these principles, put them into practice, master yourself, and become fearless.

I have taken 82 sayings from the I Ching and expanded on them. At the end of each saying and commentary, I have listed all of the related emotional competencies. There is also a table in the back of the book where the competencies and all associated sayings are listed.

How to use this book:

Step 1: Take the mini Emotional intelligence test on the following pages and graph your results.

Step 2: Evaluate your results. Which typical profile or pairings do you possess? Are these patterns or profiles problematic for you? If the answer is yes, you can choose emotional competencies that will help you to overcome these issues. We have suggested competencies to work on for each typical profile.

Step 3: Choose the emotional competencies that you will work to develop.

Step 4: Visit the table in the back of the book and find the competencies that you are going to improve. If you see an "h" by the number listed, it means that if this competency is too high, it can be problematic.

Step 5: Read an I Ching saying per day and make that saying the focus for your day. Remember to apply the sayings in the context of improving the emotional competence.

Step 6: Download our app, Tao of Emotional Intelligence. It will automatically choose a saying for you based on the competency you have chosen.

Mini Emotional Intelligence Test

Work your way through the test, then read through the interpretive guidelines for the various typical profiles and pairings of competencies. Then, read through how these typical profiles affect the different areas of your life and work.

EMOTIONAL / SOCIAL INTELLIGENCE - SNAPSHOT ASSESSMENT

Read the statement and put an "X" in the appropriate box. Use your gut level, first reaction. When you have finished, go to the end of the evaluation for directions on scoring and some interpretive guidelines for your results.

Emotional and Social Skills	STRONGLY AGREE(SA)	AGREE (A)	NEUTRAL (N)	DISAGREE (D)	STRONGLY DISAGREE(SD)
POINT VALUE	5	4	3	2	1
1. I have a healthy level of self-respect.					
2. I'm comfortable with my general appearance.					
3. If someone criticizes me, I'm able to put their feedback into perspective and keep my emotional balance.					
4. I make it a habit to take time for personal and professional development					
5. My plans for the future are motivating and energizing.					
6. It's easy for me to stay active doing those things that I find most fulfilling.					

	Emotional and Social Skills	STRONGLY AGREE(SA)	AGREE (A)	NEUTRAL (N)	DISAGREE (D)	STRONGLY DISAGRE(SD)
7.	My emotional life is rich and varied.					
8.	I'm in touch with the way I feel in most situations.					
9.	I'm seldom, if ever, 'hijacked' or caught off guard by my emotional responses to situations.					
10.	I easily express my feelings.					
11.	I enjoy showing my feelings to others.					
12.	People tell me they always know how I feel about things.					
13.	I am able to express my needs and opinions to others.					
14.	I let others know when I believe they are ignoring my rights in a situation.					
15.	I believe that expressing my honest opinion is important in maintaining good relationships.					
16.	I prefer to make my own decisions.					
17.	When working alone, I maintain a sure sense of purpose and direction.					

	Emotional and Social Skills	STRONGLY AGREE(SA)	AGREE (A)	NEUTRAL (N)	DISAGREE (D)	STRONGLY DISAGRE(SD)
18.	When working with others, I take the initiative on independent projects.					
19.	I am comfortable sharing my deep feelings with good friends.					
20.	My life is enriched by family and close friends.					
21.	Others feel comfortable confiding in me.					
22.	I'm good at discerning the way other people perceive their situations, even if different from mine.					
23.	I easily tune into the feelings of others around me in order to assess the 'emotional climate' of any group.					
24.	I appreciate it when people treat others with respect and kindness.					
25.	Helping others outside my immediate family and group of friends is important to me.					
26.	I impress others as dependable and reliable.					
27.	It's not in my nature to take advantage of others.					
28.	When confronted by a new challenge, I define and strategize different approaches.					

	Emotional and Social Skills	STRONGLY AGREE(SA)	AGREE (A)	NEUTRAL (N)	DISAGREE (D)	STRONGLY DISAGREE(SD)
29.	I generally engage in a process of evaluating the pros and cons of different approaches to resolving a problem.					
30.	I take time to collect relevant information before evaluating different ways to solve a problem.					
31.	I'm aware of how my thoughts and beliefs impact my evaluation of circumstances.					
32.	I learn about different aspects of any issue or problem before taking action.					
33.	I like to double check my facts to ensure the accuracy of assumptions.					
34.	I'm not quick to anger or hot-headed.					
35.	I am steady, patient and focused in achieving goals.					
36.	I don't give in easily to temptations or distractions.					
37.	It's my nature to remain balanced and calm even when things don't go as planned.					
38.	Others tell me that I deal well with change.					
39.	I am energized by the excitement, even the uncertainty, of beginning a new project.					

Emotional and Social Skills	STRONGLY AGREE(SA)	AGREE (A)	NEUTRAL (N)	DISAGREE (D)	STRONGLY DISAGRE(SD)
40. I usually calm down quickly after a crisis has passed.					
41. I seldom get annoyed or stressed out by events.					
42. People look to me for calm assurance and guidance when things get tough.					
43. I move forward with confidence despite setbacks					
44. I am confident about my ability to handle the unexpected.					
45. In my experience, disappointments, in the longer term, are just stepping stones to success in disguise.					
46. I'm an upbeat person who enjoys life.					
47. People consider me uplifting and fun.					
48. I'm seldom, if ever, depressed or 'down' about things.					

DIRECTIONS

For each competence below, go to the statements listed and add up your total results for those three statements. **For each 3-statement competency:**

- If you scored **3-9 total**, this is probably an area that <u>needs improvement</u>.

- If you scored **10-11 total**, your score is better, but still indicates you'd <u>likely benefit from improvement.</u>

- If you scored **12-13 total**, you are probably in the <u>average range</u>.

- If you scored **14-15 total**, you are probably <u>above average</u> in this area.

Often the most revealing aspect of this assessment is the degrees of difference between different scores, an amazingly helpful indicator of performance and behavior. Graph your results on the graph page.

SELF-PERCEPTION

Self-Regard *(Statements 1-3)* is respecting oneself while understanding and accepting one's strengths and weaknesses. Self-regard is often associated with feelings of inner strength and self-confidence.

Total points: _____

Self-Actualization *(Statements 4-6)* is the willingness to persistently try to improve oneself and engage in the pursuit of personally relevant and meaningful objectives that lead to a rich and enjoyable life.

Total points: _____

Emotional Self-Awareness *(Statements 7-9)* includes recognizing and understanding one's own emotions. This includes the ability to differentiate between subtleties in one's own emotions while understanding the cause of these emotions and the impact they have on the thoughts and actions of oneself and others.

Total points: _____

SELF EXPRESSION

Emotional Expression *(Statements 10-12)* is openly expressing one's feelings verbally and non-verbally.

Total points: _____

Assertiveness *(Statements 13-15)* involves communicating feelings, beliefs, and thoughts openly, and defending personal rights and values in a socially acceptable, non-offensive, and non-destructive manner.

Total points: _____

Independence *(Statements 16-18)* is the ability to be self-directed and free of emotional dependency on others. Decision-making, planning, and daily tasks are completed autonomously.

Total points: _____

INTERPERSONAL

Interpersonal Relationship *(Statements 19-21)* refers to the skill of developing and maintaining mutually satisfying relationships that are characterized by trust and compassion.

Total points: _____

Empathy *(Statements 22-24)* is recognizing, understanding, and appreciating how other people feel. Empathy involves being able to articulate your understanding of another's perspective and behaving in a way that respects the feelings of others.

Total points: _____

Social Responsibility *(Statements 25-27)* is willingly contributing to society, to one's social groups, and generally to the welfare of others. Social Responsibility involves acting responsibly, having social consciousness, and showing concern for the greater community.

Total points: _____

DECISION MAKING

Problem Solving *(Statements 28-30)* is the ability to find solutions to problems in situations where emotions are involved. Problem solving includes the ability to understand how emotions impact decision making.

Total points: _____

Reality Testing *(Statements 31-33)* is the capacity to remain objective by seeing things as they really are. This capacity involves recognizing when emotions or personal bias can cause one to be less objective.

Total points: _____

Impulse Control (*Statements 34-36)* is the ability to resist or delay an impulse, drive, or temptation to act. It involves avoiding rash behaviors and decision making.

Total points: _____

STRESS MANAGEMENT

Flexibility *(Statements 37-39)* is adapting emotions, thoughts, and behaviors to unfamiliar, unpredictable, and dynamic circumstances or ideas.

Total points: _____

Stress Tolerance *(Statements 40-42)* involves coping with stressful

or difficult situations and believing that one can manage or
influence situations in a positive manner.

Total points: _____

Optimism *(Statements 43-45)* is an indicator of one's positive
attitude and outlook on life. It includes remaining hopeful and
resilient, despite occasional setbacks.

Total points: _____

WELL BEING INDICATOR

Happiness *(Statements 46-48)* is the ability to feel satisfied with
one's life, to enjoy oneself and others, and to have fun.

Total points: _____

Note: Although this evaluation may give an indication of areas
which need improvement, it should not be used for in-depth,
personal development. In order to do that, we recommend that
you take the Emotional Quotient Inventory (EQ-i) 2.0, the
validated and most widely-used emotional intelligence evaluation
in the world. You can then obtain feedback on your results from a
qualified, certified emotional intelligence professional.

GRAPHING YOUR RESULTS FOR ANALYSIS / DISCUSSION

	3	4	5	6	7	8	9	10	11	12	13	14	15
SELF-PERCEPTION													
Self-Regard													
Self-Actualization													
Emotional Self-Awareness													
SELF-EXPRESSION													
Emotional Expression													
Assertiveness													
Independence													
INTERPERSONAL													
Interpersonal Relationship													
Empathy													
Social Responsibility													
DECISION MAKING													
Problem Solving													
Reality Testing													
Impulse Control													
STRESS MANAGEMENT													
Flexibility													
Stress Tolerance													
Optimism													
WELL BEING INDICATOR													
Happiness													

Once you have graphed your results, it may be helpful to place an "h" next to your three high scores and an "l" next to your three low scores. Use these highs and lows when you look at the interpretive guidelines on the following pages.

INTERPRETIVE GUIDELINES

It is desirable to have a balanced emotional profile. Avoid the trap of thinking that a high number is good and a low number is bad. Any strength taken to the extreme may become a weakness, especially if the balancing competency is low. For example: assertiveness is a great leadership skill, but if it is high and empathy is low, you may be perceived as someone who doesn't listen, doesn't ask for input or opinions, and is a know-it-all. Look at the highs and lows of your EQi and see the following descriptions of the way people may perceive you.

SELF PERCEPTION COMPOSITE

SELF-REGARD
High: Arrogant, full of yourself.
Low: Shy, lack confidence.

SELF-ACTUALIZATION

High: Have a clear plan for your future, feel good about the direction of your life.

Low: No plan, aimless, no clear vision for future, unhappy in present situation, you may see no way out.

EMOTIONAL SELF AWARENESS

High: Overly sensitive to comments, to others, and possibly to your environment.

Low: Unaware of others, your surroundings, and even your body, you "check out" often.

SELF EXPRESSION COMPOSITE

EMOTIONAL EXPRESSION

High: Easy to win the trust of those who appreciate exuberant expressiveness, though may alienate those who are more reserved.

Low: The opposite: more likely to fail to connect with those who are expressive - but generally better received by emotionally reserved types.

ASSERTIVENESS

High: Bowl people over, don't take into account others' feelings or input - often perceived as aggressive.

Low: Don't speak what is on your mind, don't stand up for yourself, aren't clear in setting expectations or declaring own needs.

INDEPENDENCE

High: Would rather work alone and be alone, not comfortable in groups or teams or social settings.

Low: Dependent on others for self worth, would rather be told what to do, thrive in groups and teams.

INTERPERSONAL COMPOSITE

INTERPERSONAL RELATIONSHIP

High: Gregarious, have a lot of friends, create instant rapport, stay in touch.

Low: Uncomfortable in social settings and meeting new people, do not stay in touch, may come across as a wallflower.

EMPATHY

High: Very sensitive to the needs of others and their feelings.

Low: Oblivious to others and their needs and feelings.

SOCIAL RESPONSIBILITY

High: Great team member, good neighbor, joiner, like to interact with groups, very social.

Low: You do not do well in groups or teams, not social; don't like to be a member of groups.

DECISION MAKING COMPOSITE

PROBLEM SOLVING

High: Able to arrive at workable solutions to problems quickly and understand how emotions can affect problem solving.

Low: You struggle with defining problems and arriving at solutions and are often overwhelmed emotionally by the problem-solving process.

REALITY TESTING

High: You see things as they really are despite emotions surrounding the situation.

Low: See all of the possibilities, do not investigate or reflect on the specific facts of a situation, live in a world where objective reality is unclear.

IMPULSE CONTROL

High: 'Paralysis of analysis,' over-thinks things, won't pull the trigger.

Low: You may have compulsive or addictive behavior such as eating, drinking, gambling, smoking, sex, spending, talking, etc., in which there is a consistent 'hijacking' of your long-term best interests - resulting in possible profound physical as well as emotional effects.

STRESS MANAGEMENT COMPOSITE

FLEXIBILITY

High: Trouble saying no, take on too much, float from one thing to the next, trouble finishing things. Physical correlation: Sugar Handling.

Low: Very rigid in your approach to things, want to maintain control.

STRESS TOLERANCE

High: Have the ability to handle a lot of stress, good coping skills. **Note:** We have found that some people with very high stress tolerance may first start to show physical signs of stress like fatigue, headaches or other pains, stomach issues, trouble sleeping, irritability, diminished sex drive, lowered immune response, and depression.

Low: Cluttered, harried, hurried, reactive, unable to stay on top of things, probably have symptoms of stress, feel overwhelmed.

OPTIMISM

High: You consistently see your future as bright and sunny, sometimes to your own detriment. - Glass half full.

Low: The curmudgeon who always looks on the dismal side of life. - Glass half empty.

WELL BEING INDICATOR

HAPPINESS:

High: Shiny, happy person who always seems to be in a good mood and full of joy.

Low: Always seem down and out, life is not fun, you find no joy,

The following are typical profiles based on emotional high and low scores. Note: with this small sampling of questions, a difference of one or two points can be significant.

If you see these relative emotional highs and lows, ESPECIALLY the underlined competencies, you may have the

SELF SACRIFICE PROFILE:

High: empathy, self awareness, interpersonal relationships, social responsibility, flexibility

Low: assertiveness, independence, emotional expression, stress tolerance, self-regard

How does this Self Sacrifice Profile affect the following?:

Time Management: Because you may not set proper limits and boundaries and are reluctant to say no, you will likely take on too much and be pulled into other people's agendas. This adds to stress levels and your work suffers.

Relationships: You may have scored lower in relationship skills because your relationships may not be mutually satisfying. You may give more than you get. Self sacrificers think that when they start setting better limits and boundaries, that people won't like them anymore. The opposite is true. These limits create clear expectations and communication.

Team Interaction: You are a great team member, but you may not speak up and contribute your ideas.

Communication: Because you may be reluctant to say what you are thinking and feeling, there may be miscommunications. You may overpromise and under-deliver because you don't want to say no.

Presentation Skills: You may be reluctant to "put yourself out there" and connect with the audience.

Stress Management: Because you say yes a lot and don't set limits, you will likely take on too much and be overwhelmed much of the time. Stress levels stay high.

Things to Work On: Assertiveness is the key to this profile. Be clear in your communications. Set better limits and boundaries. Begin each day with YOUR list of things to accomplish and don't be pulled off track by others. Have times when your door is closed. When these communications are clear, there is a deeper level of understanding.

If you see these relative emotional highs and lows, ESPECIALLY the underlined competencies, you may have the

ALPHA PROFILE:

High: <u>assertiveness</u>, self regard, and/or independence

Low: <u>empathy</u>, self awareness, social responsibility, interpersonal relationships, impulse control, emotional expression, flexibility

Note: Alphas also tend to have the Control/Puppet Master/ Perfectionist profile. See the next pages for that profile definition.

How does this Alpha Profile affect the following?:

Time Management: You may take on way too much because you don't think anyone can do it as well as you can. You may have trouble delegating.

Relationships: Doesn't listen, doesn't ask for opinions or input from others. Takes charge, takes over. If coupled with high self regard, may be seen as arrogant.

Team Interaction: Has a tendency to take over and not work in a collaborative way.

Communication: Poor listening skills. Lack of understanding of others and their needs.

Presentation Skills: Usually good presenters, but lower empathy prevents a connection with the audience and understanding what they want.

Stress Management: Alphas are frequently stressed and hurried. They rarely take the time for themselves or build in daily reflection and recovery time.

Things to Work On: Empathy is a big key for alphas. By tuning in more to the needs of others, you create more intimate connections with others, which will help with your success both personally and professionally.

Abrasive: A sub-profile of the Alpha Profile

For alphas, if you see a difference of 2 to 4 points or more between assertiveness and empathy, you may be perceived as abrasive, abrupt, and without tact. You likely don't listen well, don't ask for opinions or input from others, and tend to take charge or take over. If coupled with high self regard, you may be seen as arrogant. At its most extreme, these ultra alphas can be seen as aggressive, abusive, or bullying.

High: Assertiveness
Low: Empathy

If you see these relative emotional highs and lows, ESPECIALLY the underlined competencies, you have the

CONTROLLER/PUPPET MASTER/PERFECTIONIST PROFILE:

<u>High</u>: <u>reality testing, problem solving</u>, impulse control
<u>Low</u>: <u>flexibility</u>

Look at self-regard. If self-regard is **low**, you may be a perfectionist who beats yourself up because you don't live up to your own standards. If self-regard is **high**, you think that no one else can do it better than you. Either wgooay, people with this profile have a hard time letting go of control and delegating. You tend to be a workaholic, but are rarely seen as a leader. **This is one of the biggest stumbling blocks to moving past a middle management position.**

How does this Control/Puppet Master/Perfectionist Profile affect the following?:

Time Management: Trouble delegating. You tend to work a lot, but never get everything done. You won't let others do things their way. You won't let them make their mistakes. You are the go to problem solver. You stay in the details.

Relationships: You may try to control too many things in relationships, which leads to conflicts. Remember, you can be right or you can be happy.

Team Interaction: You tend to try and control the process and control the direction of the team. Negatively affects collaboration and the team process.

Communication: Preconceptions on how things should be may prevent understanding and connection with others.

Presentation Skills: May be rigid in your approach to presenting. Try being more spontaneous and improvisational. You don't have to have a perfect speech.

Stress Management: Overwhelmed because of lack of delegation. Works too much. Wants to be in on all decisions and know all information and details.

Things to Work On: Flexibility: with yourself, with others, with outcomes. By having a more flexible approach. Delegate more. Ask yourself: Is it wrong, or is it just different? Also, better stress tolerance can be helpful.

If you see these relative emotional highs and lows, ESPECIALLY the underlined competencies, you may have the

ANGER, FRUSTRATION, IMPATIENCE PROFILE:

High: Assertiveness,

Low: Impulse Control, Flexibility

How does this Anger, Frustration, Impatience Profile affect the following?:

Time Management: When experiencing anger, your thinking brain shuts down. This cognitive impairment reduces efficiency.

Relationships: Explosions directed toward others creates negative experiences and diminishes relationships. People won't come to you with anything negative for fear of an explosion.

Team Interaction: Team members may not connect with you. Your explosive nature diminishes interactions.

Communication: Anger, frustration, and impatience limits your communication skills. People will avoid you and not share information because of you over-reactions.

Presentation Skills: May have trouble settling into a calm, easy presentation.

Stress Management: This is a huge factor that adds to stress levels. You are in a low level fight or flight most of your day, which wears you out. By the end of the day, you are likely exhausted.

Things to Work On: Work on impulse control and empathy. Empathy will decrease assertiveness and impulse control will help with the reactions. Remember, respond instead of react.

If you see these relative emotional lows, you may have the

BURNOUT PROFILE:

Low: self-regard, interpersonal relationships, self-actualization, stress tolerance, optimism

Four or five out of five = total burnout. Three out of five = highly stressed. Two out of five = pay attention. These five competencies contribute to an overall level of happiness and well being. Your happiness score may be low as well.

Low **stress tolerance** indicates an inability to handle stressful situations, especially when there are strong emotions involved. You feel overwhelmed and hurried.

How does this Burnout Profile affect the following?:

Time Management: Don't have the energy to get all of your work done. Overwhelmed, in fight or flight, cognitive processes impaired.

Relationships: Very little time and energy for the relationships in your life and work. May come across as withdrawn and disinterested.

Team Interaction: In survival mode, don't create connections and interactions, also too tired to contribute, you do the minimum.

Communication: Cognitive impairment reduces communication ability. Also, because you are exhausted, you may come across as disinterested.

Presentation Skills: Great presentation is all about energy. When your energy is low, there is no connection with the audience.

Stress Management: Self explanatory.

Things to Work On: Stress Management is a key here. Build in recovery throughout your day. In addition, if your emotional self-awareness is low, that is the place to begin. You must be able to identify when you are tired, overwhelmed, etc. You must know what is happening in your body.

Racing Toward Burnout, a Sub-Profile of the Burnout Profile:

NOTE: If you have high stress tolerance, but also are experiencing the physical symptoms of stress (trouble sleeping, headaches or other pain, fatigue, stomach problems, diminished immunity: frequents colds or flu, diminished sex drive, diminished cognitive ability, melancholy or depression) you are racing toward burnout. Just because you have the capacity to cope with stress emotionally doesn't mean it's not taking its toll on your body.

If you see these relative emotional highs and lows, ESPECIALLY the underlined competencies, you may have the

CHAOS, REACTIVE MANAGEMENT PROFILE:

High: Stress Tolerance

Low: Impulse Control

How does this Chaos/Reactive Management Profile affect the following?:

Time Management: You get a lot done, but are just reacting to things. You do not plan proactively. You will usually have low problem-solving skills as well. Work place usually cluttered and cramped.

Relationships: No time for meaningful relationships. Reacts to everything.

Team Interaction: Living in a world of chaos, team interactions are usually frantic and frazzled.

Communication: You don't take the time to cultivate relationships. You may be trying to check emails and work while you are interacting with others.

Presentation Skills: Disorganization contributes to poor presentations.

Stress Management: Always feeling behind, on the treadmill. Feeling stress constantly.

Things to Work On: Increase impulse control while working on managing stress. Remember, respond instead of react.

OVERLY OPTIMISTIC PROFILE: Glass half full

High: Optimism

Low: Reality Testing

How does this Overly Optimistic Profile affect the following?:

Time Management: You think you can get more done than you actually can, so you tend to try to schedule too much.

Relationships: People like to be around optimistic, upbeat people. Sometimes over-commitment can lead to misunderstandings and not honoring promises.

Team Interaction: Unrealistic expectations that cannot be met.

Communication: May over-reach with expectations and not communicate clearly with details.

Presentation Skills: Good for presenting. Optimistic, upbeat energy is a magnet.

Stress Management: Mostly good for stress management. Optimistic people tend to cope with stress better, but over-committing and taking on too much may add to stress.

Things to Work On: Would benefit from reality checks with someone you trust. Try to temper your optimism with reality checks.

PESSIMIST OR REALIST PROFILE: **Glass half empty**

High: Reality Testing

Low: Optimism

How does this Pessimist Profile affect the following?:

Time Management: Negative attitude may reduce performance and results. May get mired down in all of the things that are impediments to progress.

Relationships: People shy away from negative people.

Team Interaction: Bring the team down. Be the curmudgeon who always looks at the negative side.

Communication: May take communications down a negative path by focusing on the negative.

Presentation Skills: Audiences may not connect with a negative presentation of a message.

Stress Management: Pessimistic people have higher levels of stress.

Things to Work On: Increase optimism and create more balance. Would benefit from reality checks with someone you trust.

TEAM PLAYER PROFILE:

High: Social Responsibility

Low: Independence

How does this Team Player profile affect the following?:

Time Management: You may take on too much for the team and not be able to complete your own work.

Relationships: Generally good at relationships, especially in a team setting.

Team Interaction: Excellent with team and collaboration. But may be reluctant to contribute your own ideas.

Communication: Your lower independence may hinder good communication if you hold back saying what is on your mind. But generally, these folks are good communicators.

Presentation Skills: Good presenters. Good connections with audiences.

Stress Management: You may take on too much, which adds to stress levels.

Things to Work On: If there is a large gap between independence and social responsibility (2 to 4 points or greater), you may want to work on independence to create some balance. Assertiveness would also be helpful to create the balance.

THE LONER PROFILE:

High: Independence

Low: Social Responsibility

Would benefit from reality checks with someone you trust. Glass half empty.

How does this Loner profile affect the following?:

Time Management: Watch isolation that may lead to overwhelm and not relying on others for help.

Relationships: Generally, relationships are not strong. Can be held back by a lack of relationships and social networks.

Team Interaction: Sometimes a good contributor, but usually behind the scenes.

Communication: Without meaningful connections and relationships, sometimes communication is on a superficial level.

Presentation Skills: Generally low energy for presentations and not a great connection with the audience.

Stress Management: Stress levels can be high, especially if you don't ask for help.

Things to Work On: Work on social responsibility and relationships (especially if there is a difference of 2 to 4 points or greater)

CHASES SHINY OBJECTS PROFILE:

High: Flexibility

Low: Impulse Control

How does this Chases Shiny Objects profile affect the following?:

Time Management: Generally cluttered work space. You start more than you finish and go from one thing to the next.

Relationships: You may come across as scattered and unfocused. This may negatively affect relationships.

Team Interaction: Scattered and unfocused, team members may not trust you to complete and contribute.

Communication: Hard to pin down. Unclear communication at times. Unfocused.

Presentation Skills: Presentations seem to be scattered. Goes down rabbit trails and loses the audience.

Stress Management: Stress levels can be high. You rarely slow down and build in recovery.

Things to Work On: Increase impulse control and assertiveness, which will reduce flexibility. Would benefit from learning rhetoric for communication and presentations.

CONTACT INFORMATION

For more information on the use of this mini Emotional Intelligence Test, contact the following:

Test devised by
Dennis Ghyst, Ph.D., Ghyst & Associates

ghyst2288@charter.net
770-438-0022
www.ghystconsulting.com

Contributions on interpretive guidelines by
Brent Darnell/Brent Darnell International
brent@brentdarnell.com
www.brentdarnell.com

Once you have determined the areas you would like to improve, go to the table in the back of the book and find the competencies listed. Then, every day, visit the sayings associated with those competencies and try to incorporate them into your day.

By focusing on these emotional competencies, and reading and studying the saying from the I Ching, you will start down the road to personal development and be able to create positive changes in your life and in your emotional makeup.

You can also use our app, Tao of Emotional Intelligence, to accomplish the same thing.

1

Wisdom Exalts

New knowledge is always difficult. We find new ideas, concepts, and ways of doing things strange. Recently, neuroscientists have verified that when you learn new things, the brain creates new neural pathways. This is an arduous process. They have verified what we already know. Change is painful and difficult. But once we gain that new knowledge, apply it, and experience success with it, we are happy and exalted. By choosing to read this book, you have already taken steps to attain new wisdom.

Related Competencies:

- Emotional Self-Awareness
- Problem Solving
- Reality Testing
- Flexibility
- Happiness

2

On the road to success, as you near the attainment of your goal, beware of becoming intoxicated with your achievement.

Many times we get full of ourselves and think that our success is totally due to our brilliance. We must have the Emotional Self-Awareness to identify this in ourselves. We must know when our Self-Regard is getting so high that it becomes a liability. Practice Emotional Self-Awareness, and when you find yourself being arrogant and complacent. Analyze and assess the situation using good Problem Solving skills. Use good Reality Testing and don't be overly optimistic.

Related Competencies:

- Self-Regard (too high)
- Emotional Self-Awareness
- Problem Solving
- Reality Testing
- Optimism (too high)

3

Exceptional modesty and conscientiousness are sure to be rewarded with great success and good fortune.

If you can keep your Self-Regard in check and be humble in your dealings with others, you will receive great rewards. People will follow you, colleagues will respect you, clients will love you. Be conscientious and complete your work to the best of your ability and don't boast about your accomplishments. You will attain your goals as the tortoise, slowly and steadily. You will not become the hare and race towards your goals, boasting all the way about yourself only to be defeated in the end.

Related Competencies:

- Self-Regard (too high)
- Emotional Self-Awareness
- Problem Solving

4

If we want to know what anyone is like, we have only to observe on what he bestows his care and what sides of his own nature he cultivates and nourishes.

Pay attention to what people hold dear and you will be able to tell much about that person. What do they value? How do they dress? What do they talk about? Where do they put their energy? Don't take this lightly. By observing all of these things you will be able to see if this is a person you want to get to know.

Related Competencies:

- Self-Actualization
- Emotional Self-Awareness
- Interpersonal Relationships
- Empathy
- Problem Solving
- Reality Testing

5

After a matter has been thoroughly considered, it is essential to form a decision and to act.

You must strike a balance between reacting and being frozen and not making a decision. Practice your Problem Solving skills and utilize your Impulse Control. Don't just react, but once you have considered all of the possibilities, then you must use your Assertiveness and act.

Related Competencies:

- Emotional Expression
- Assertiveness
- Impulse Control
- Problem Solving

6

If you live in a state of perpetual hurry, you will fail to attain inner composure.

If you are in a constant state of agitation and impulsiveness, you will not be able to make good decisions. You must practice quieting your mind with reflection time in the form of prayer or meditation. You must practice centering techniques such as mindfulness and deep breathing in order to calm your mind and enable you to think clearly. When you are focused and centered, good decisions are made. The superior person practices some form of meditation to be able to focus when necessary.

Related Competencies:

- Problem Solving
- Impulse Control
- Stress Tolerance

7

Unlimited possibilities are not suited to mankind. If they existed, his life would only dissolve into the boundless.

Modern life is continuously accelerating, giving us unlimited possibilities. This may be detrimental to us. Working within limits gives us comfort makes us more effective. The superior person recognizes the value of limits. He uses focus to avoid being paralyzed by limitless possibilities. He does not spend his time flitting from one thing to the next in this sea of infinity, but focuses his effort like a laser beam for maximum results.

Related Competencies:

- Self-Actualization
- Emotional Self-Awareness
- Impulse Control
- Flexibility (too high)
- Happiness

8

A situation only becomes favorable when one adapts to it.

When bad things happen, we tend to dwell on it. When people act unreasonably, we tend to wish they were different. We resist the situation, we defend, we justify, we work like hell to reverse it. We act in a totally reactive mode. But the superior person realizes that all situations happen for a reason, and he looks for the advantage immediately. He does not dwell on the situation or fight against it, but tries to use the circumstances to his best advantage. You cannot control the situation, and you cannot control others. But you have 100% control of your response. The next time something happens to you that seems to be a disadvantage, act as though it is for your benefit. Find the positive in it. Use the situation to learn and grow. Whenever there is resistance, there is an opportunity to learn. The superior person takes the path of learning.

Related Competencies:

- Problem Solving
- Reality Testing
- Impulse Control
- Flexibility
- Optimism

9

If you are not dazzled by enticing goals, and remain true to yourself, you will travel through life unassailed, on a level road.

You may be enticed by a certain job offer or position, a way to get rich quickly, a way to move ahead without work, a way to get ahead that compromises your values. Don't be sucked into this trap. Take a look at the reality of the situation. Remember: if it sounds too good to be true, it probably is. The superior person knows that any gains made on this path will not last. Walk in the way of the superior person and maintain your integrity and honesty. Work hard and be diligent in your approach to success. There is no substitute for hard work and constant improvement. Then, when you reach a level of success, you are truly happy and content with your position.

Related Competencies:

- Self-Actualization
- Reality Testing
- Impulse Control
- Happiness

10

When confronted with insurmountable forces retreat is proper.

Some people don't know when to admit defeat. There is a real virtue in the United States to never give up. This is admirable, but can be detrimental. Sometimes, our egos prevent us from retreating even though it is the proper thing to do. Sometimes, we don't give into the other person at the cost of the relationship. Sometimes, we are overly optimistic and don't take the proper action until it is too late. The superior person knows when to retreat and re-group. He is flexible with his original plans and knows when they should be scrapped. He conserves his resources and builds his strength, making plans for the next battle.

Related Competencies:

- Self-Regard (too high)
- Problem Solving
- Reality Testing
- Flexibility
- Optimism (too high)

11

The superior person spends a lifetime developing strong character, and so enjoys a lifetime of supreme good fortune and great success.

In our fast-paced work world with our reactive management style, we seldom find the time to develop ourselves. Between work and family, there is little time left for ourselves. We put work first, then family, then ourselves. The superior person goes against this conventional wisdom and takes care of himself first. For the superior person knows that if he loses himself, he is no good to his employer or his family. Develop strong character. Control your impulses to accept the status quo. Take classes, read books, watch less TV, travel more, learn new things, cultivate new relationships, constantly be on the lookout for things that will improve who you are. In this way, you will learn about balance and cultivate success in everything that you do.

Related Competencies:

- Self-Actualization
- Emotional Self-Awareness
- Interpersonal Relationships
- Impulse Control
- Stress Tolerance
- Happiness

12

If you attempt too much, you will end by succeeding in nothing.

We value hard work and long hours. We want to be Superman and never say no to our superiors. We have the attitude that nothing is impossible. We want to take on the world and be the workhorses that get amazing results. But the superior person knows when to say no and how to set limits. He knows how to focus his efforts and prioritize his work to get the maximum results with the least effort. Take a look at those people who have great life balance. They seem to do everything well and they seem to get so much done. It's because they have learned to set proper limits and define the things that are truly important. Take a look at those people who take on too much. They are stressed out and on the verge of burnout. That is not the path of the superior person.

Related Competencies:

- Self-Actualization
- Problem Solving
- Reality Testing
- Impulse Control
- Flexibility (too high)
- Stress Tolerance
- Happiness

13

The small-minded person is not ashamed of unkindness and does not shrink from injustice.

When you see injustice and unfairness, do you turn the other way or do you fight for what is right? The superior person concerns himself with justice and right because he knows that because we are all inter-connected, if something is done unfairly to someone else, it is done unfairly to him. Injustice diminishes everyone in society. Fight for what is right.

Related Competencies:

- Emotional Self-Awareness
- Assertiveness
- Independence
- Interpersonal Relationships
- Empathy
- Social Responsibility
- Flexibility (too high)

14

In financial matters, well-being prevails when expenditures and income are in proportion.

The superior person knows that when his spending is in line with his income, there is harmony and prosperity. The superior person doesn't become a slave to credit. He controls his impulses to buy. He uses the 24-hour rule where he sleeps on potential purchases instead of impulsively buying. He creates a budget and sticks with it. He saves for his purchases and only borrows when it is warranted. Thus, he avoids debt and creates a life filled with happiness. He also avoids the stress of debt, which is constantly hanging over his head.

Related Competencies:

- Impulse Control
- Stress Tolerance
- Happiness

15

In cultivating oneself, it is best to root out bad habits and tolerate those that are harmless.

The superior person will work on aspects of himself that are not desirable and try to make them better. But he also knows that minor infractions should be tolerated. If he is working on Impulse Control and avoided buying a new car that he really didn't need, but on the way home stopped off for an ice cream, this is a harmless lapse in Impulse Control and is perfectly fine. He has the Emotional Self-Awareness and Reality Testing to understand the differences in these two circumstances. By cultivating oneself, the superior person will lead a life filled with Self-Actualization and Happiness.

Related Competencies:

- Self-Actualization
- Emotional Self-Awareness
- Reality Testing
- Impulse Control
- Happiness

16

A compromise with evil is not possible.

When we encounter people that are simply evil-minded, we continually wish that they were different. We must develop our Empathy skills to know the hearts of others. We must also accept that they will likely never change. In those cases, we must do what we know is right and not give in to their approaches. They may want us to delve into the gray area. We must resist temptation to do that and continue on the right path. Do not be overcome by evil, but overcome evil with good.

Related Competencies:

- Assertiveness
- Independence
- Empathy
- Reality Testing
- Impulse Control

17

Once you have gained inner mastery of a problem, it will come about naturally that the action you take will succeed.

Remember that all problems are opportunities to improve. Study the problem with that in mind, knowing that the action you take will strengthen you. Also know that no matter what action you take, it will be the right one. Even if there is failure, there is learning. Don't be paralyzed by analysis. Go forward with a positive attitude knowing that no matter what happens, you will come out victorious.

Related Competencies:

- Emotional Expression
- Assertiveness
- Problem Solving
- Optimism

18

Knowledge is the key to freedom.

Your accumulation of knowledge gives you freedom and power. Your technical knowledge allows you to keep a good position at work and provide for your family. Knowledge of good work/life balance frees you from stress and burnout. Self-knowledge makes you free from fear. Knowing the right path will free you from misfortune and failure. Be independent in your thinking and develop a continual thirst for knowledge. The more you know, the more you are set free.

Related Competencies:

- Self-Regard
- Emotional Self-Awareness
- Independence
- Problem Solving
- Stress Tolerance

19

In general, opposition appears as an obstruction, but the superior person uses it to his advantage.

When we encounter opposition, our first reaction is to fight, to defend, to justify. But the superior person knows that this opposition is a chance to practice Emotional Self-Awareness and empathy to learn about himself and others. He does not groan about his bad misfortune, he does not resist, but goes forward with confidence armed with optimism and the ability to deal with the situation in a positive way. He knows this could be a great opportunity. Innovation comes out of necessity. Adversity builds us up and hones us. Forged in the fires of adversity, we emerge tempered and strong.

Related Competencies:

- Self-Regard
- Self-Actualization
- Emotional Self-Awareness
- Assertiveness
- Empathy
- Problem Solving
- Impulse Control
- Stress Tolerance

20

Do not set your eyes on the harvest while planting it, nor on the use of ground while clearing it.

You must be totally in the moment and self-aware at all times. Use your Impulse Control and don't let your mind go toward the future too quickly. Too much Optimism without the balance of Reality Testing will lead to failure. Don't be overly Optimistic about future events. Use your Problem Solving skills to take care of the present.

Related Competencies:

- Emotional Self-Awareness
- Problem Solving
- Reality Testing
- Impulse Control
- Optimism (too high)

21

In times of prosperity it is important to possess enough greatness of spirit to bear with the mistakes of others.

This is a great leadership skill. We have a tendency to be inflexible and shoot the messenger. But what does this create? If you don't have a good sense of the reality of the situation, if you react and come down hard on people who bring their mistakes to your attention, in the future, they will try to hide their mistakes. This could lead to disastrous consequences. Use your Empathy skills. Imagine how hard it was for this person to bring this situation to your attention. The superior person controls his impulses and uses his Flexibility, forgiving even intentional variations from the right path. He uses this situation to teach others, solve future problems, and build better relationships and teams. By coming down hard on others, you will create resentment and disharmony among the team and put your prosperity in jeopardy.

Related Competencies:
- Emotional Self-Awareness
- Assertiveness (too high)
- Interpersonal Relationships
- Empathy
- Social Responsibility
- Problem Solving
- Reality Testing
- Impulse Control
- Flexibility

22

If you neglect your good qualities and virtues, you will cease to be of value to your friends and neighbors. Soon, no one will seek you out or bother about you.

The superior person is constantly looking for ways to improve himself. He is constantly learning and cultivating relationships for the greater good. The inferior person is ultimately left to his own devices because no one wants to be around him. Seek to cultivate all that is good in you, then seek out that same good in others. Together, you will strive for the good of the group.

Related Competencies:

- Interpersonal Relationships
- Social Responsibility

23

To be successful, do not be rigid and immobile in your thinking, but always keep abreast of the time and change with it.

Low Flexibility is the source of much misfortune. Look at the story of the oak tree and the reed. During a storm, the mighty oak dug in and became as rigid as he could, and the wind finally destroyed him. The reed was flexible, bent with the wind, and survived the storm. Cultivate Flexibility in all that you do. In your principles, do not be moved, but in your dealings with yourself and others, cultivate a flexible nature. This will lead to great success.

Related Competencies:

- Interpersonal Relationships
- Problem Solving
- Reality Testing
- Flexibility

24

A superior person acquaints himself with many sayings of antiquity and many deeds of the past, and thus strengthens his character.

If we do not learn from history, we are doomed to repeat it. The superior person taps into the great storehouse of wisdom that is available. He increases his Emotional Self-Awareness, strength of character, and Self-Regard. He stays on the right path toward his goals. He sees the reality of the situation by learning from those who have been through the same thing. One way to do this is to set aside "sacred time" each day to read and study the great books of wisdom such as the Tao Te Ching, the Bible, The Bhagavad Gita, The Vedas, or the Koran.

Related Competencies:

- Self-Regard
- Self-Actualization
- Emotional Self-Awareness
- Problem Solving
- Reality Testing

25

By manifesting a humble attitude, people will naturally want to help you and give you good counsel.

By keeping your Self-Regard in check and not becoming arrogant, you will open the door for others to help you. Most people love to help, but arrogance will drive them away. Cultivate your Empathy skills by allowing others to help. Cultivate the relationship skills necessary to collaborate with others.

Related Competencies:

- Self-Regard (too high)
- Emotional Expression
- Emotional Self-Awareness
- Interpersonal Relationships
- Empathy
- Social Responsibility

26

Waiting should not be mere empty hoping; it should be filled with the inner certainty of reaching the goal.

If you worry about failure, you will be more likely to fail. The superior person plans and prepares and has confidence in the future and the attainment of his goals. Being optimistic creates happy thoughts and positive energy which leads to the attainment of your goals.

Related Competencies:

- Self-Regard
- Self-Actualization
- Optimism
- Happiness

27

It is better to go on foot than ride in a carriage under false pretenses.

The superior person does not put on airs. He lives within his means and knows his place. He does not pretend to be something he is not. He does not present a false image. He is real and open and honest. This creates close relationships and honorable character. The inferior person does not have good Self-Regard and must resort to building himself up falsely in order to feel good about himself. This will lead to disaster and loss of respect.

Related Competencies:

- Self-Regard
- Self-Actualization
- Interpersonal Relationships
- Reality Testing

28

If you would have your relationships endure, fix your mind on an end that endures.

Every relationship has its problems. There are arguments, misunderstandings, miscommunications, and disagreements. If you both make a commitment to work hard and maintain the relationship, you can overcome all of these problems. Even the best relationships are difficult at times. But if you fix your mind on keeping the relationship no matter what, the relationship will endure.

Related Competencies:

- Self-Actualization
- Interpersonal Relationships
- Optimism
- Happiness

29

Do not hate. Hatred is a form of subjective involvement that binds you to the hated object.

You think that when you hate something, you dismiss it from your life, but the opposite is true. When you hate, you are connected to that object in a profound and lasting way. The only way you can be free of this object and the negativity surrounding the hatred is to forgive and to send love and tolerance to the object. Use your Empathy to try and see their point of view. This frees you from the hatred and the negativity. Hatred is fear. By being secure in yourself, you release that fear. By keeping your Assertiveness in check, you do not become aggressive, but are content and happy.

Related Competencies:

- Emotional Expression
- Assertiveness
- Empathy
- Impulse Control
- Happiness

30

The superior person is never led into baseness or vulgarity by community of interests with people of low character.

We used to call it peer pressure, and we think that, as adults, we are over it. But there is still the possibility to be led astray by others. We must be vigilant and have confidence in ourselves. We must be self-aware so as not to fall into this trap. We must use our Impulse Control and think situations through before participating. We must be independent thinkers.

Related Competencies:

- Self-Regard
- Emotional Self-Awareness
- Independence
- Impulse Control

31

The superior person is reverent; at all times acknowledging the great Creator and the wondrousness of the universe.

The superior person is aware that there is a higher power out there, something greater than ourselves. This knowledge creates awe, wonder, contentment, and happiness. The superior person is also optimistic about the future not only for this life, but for what lies after death.

Related Competencies:

- Emotional Expression
- Optimism
- Happiness

32

Boasting of power, wealth, position, promotion, success, or influential friends inevitably invites misfortune and humiliation.

Pride cometh before a fall. If we don't keep our Self-Regard in check, we are headed for disaster. The superior person cultivates humility and relies on others. This ensures his continued success.

Related Competencies:

- Self-Regard (too high)
- Emotional Expression
- Interpersonal Relationships

33

Only through daily self-renewal of character can you continue at the height of your powers.

Life is hectic and busy. We get off track. We fall into bad habits and patterns. Only by keeping an eye on things do we prevent this. You must have a plan, you must work your plan, you must have accountability and follow-up, and you must check in and tweak your plan at least once a year. It is also a good idea to build in daily reflection time to check in. Crave to learn as you crave air to breathe. Strive to continually improve yourself. This will ensure success in everything that you do.

Related Competencies:

- Self-Actualization
- Emotional Self-Awareness
- Stress Tolerance
- Happiness

34

To a person of true understanding it makes no difference whether death comes early or late.

You have only around 4,000 weeks here on this earth. The superior person uses his time wisely and productively. He is aware, in the moment, and enjoys life to the fullest. He sucks the marrow out of life and cultivates good work/life balance. He is full of life and energy. To the superior person, death is just a transition. What you do while you are here prepares you for that transition and ensures your earthly success.

Related Competencies:

- Self-Actualization
- Emotional Self-Awareness
- Impulse Control
- Stress Tolerance
- Optimism
- Happiness

35

Only a person who goes to meet his fate resolutely will be equipped to deal with it adequately.

The superior person lets nothing stand in his way. He accepts his fate as it comes and makes the best of any situation. He is determined and resolute that he will prevail. There is no delusion. He sees the real situation and faces it head on.

Related Competencies:

- Self-Actualization
- Assertiveness
- Problem Solving
- Reality Testing

36

It is only after perfect balance has been achieved that any misstep brings imbalance.

Once we have a level of success, we are always afraid that it will be short lived. The inferior person hordes his treasures and lives in fear. But the superior person knows that everything is transitory. They know that they are not defined by their success and that they will be able to deal with whatever comes their way. Therefore, they do not live in fear, but are optimistic about the future.

Related Competencies:

- Self-Actualization
- Stress Tolerance
- Optimism

37

When entangled in a conflict it is wise to remain so clear headed and strong that you are always ready to come to terms with your opponent by meeting him halfway.

During conflict, your opponent is trying to harm you. By being flexible and willing to meet your opponent half way, you save your energy and resources. This leads to a time without conflict, where you can be happy and plan for the future. To refuse to meet an opponent half way and fighting until the bitter end only inflicts harm to both parties and prevents us from moving forward in a positive way.

Related Competencies:

- Emotional Expression
- Interpersonal Relationships
- Empathy
- Problem Solving
- Reality Testing
- Impulse Control
- Flexibility

38

Even the finest clothes turn to rags.

Everything is in a state of decay. Everything is evolving into something else. All that is will eventually be no more. The superior person acknowledges the transitory nature of life and cultivates those things that endure such as character, honor, integrity, and virtue. Honor your possessions, but don't become a slave to them. They are turning to dust as you read this.

Related Competencies:

- Self-Actualization
- Reality Testing

39

If you see good, imitate it. If you have faults, rid yourself of them.

The superior person is constantly looking for ways to improve himself. He reads, he learns, he takes classes. This leads to confidence and success. He does not give in to impulses, but cultivates Emotional Self-Awareness. By using Empathy, he can see what is good in others and learn from them.

Related Competencies:

- Self-Regard
- Emotional Self-Awareness
- Empathy
- Impulse Control

40

In order to achieve a quiet heart, rest and movement must follow each other in accordance with the demands of the time.

We are a working nation. We value hard work. But we tend to work too much, and it is causing our nation much distress. Burnout is reaching epidemic proportions. Deaths from heart disease and other stress-related illnesses are rising. The superior person knows that he must learn to rest after working hard. He strives for good work/life balance. He builds in recovery activities throughout the day. He takes his vacations. He has good time management skills so that he works efficiently.

Related Competencies:

- Emotional Self-Awareness
- Impulse Control
- Stress Tolerance

41

If you depend on your relationships for your happiness, you will either be happy or sad as your relationships rise and fall.

The superior person is able to be comfortable with himself and enjoys his time alone. He can enjoy the company of others, but is not dependent on that company for his happiness. By cultivating good Self-Regard and Independence, there is no danger.

Related Competencies:

- Self-Regard
- Independence

42

To act on the spur of every caprice, ultimately leads to humiliation.

The inferior person runs from desire to desire without thinking. He reacts impulsively to every situation. The superior person realizes that to control himself is the ultimate wisdom. He does not impulsively run after people that may benefit him, he does not obey every order given him without question, and he does not run after relationships based on his mood at the time. Controlling yourself will lead to success and happiness.

Related Competencies:

- Emotional Expression
- Impulse Control
- Flexibility (too high)

43

No plain is not followed by a slope, no increase is not followed by a decrease.

Everything goes in cycles: the tides, the economy, planetary motion, fads, the list is endless. The superior person knows this law and during times of prosperity, he prepares for recession. In times of wellness, he prepares for illness. That way, he is always prepared for the downturn. This will ensure great fortune and success.

Related Competencies:

- Self-Actualization
- Problem Solving
- Reality Testing
- Impulse Control
- Flexibility

44

It is wise and reasonable not to try to obtain anything by force.

The inferior person will use his strength and authority (high Assertiveness) to force people into submission. But this only brings about resentment and disharmony. In addition, anything taken by force must be maintained by force. This is a drain on energy and resources. This will lead to regret and failure. The superior person knows how to obtain the things he needs by cooperation and by cultivating great relationships. He uses his Empathy skills to understand others and their needs. He never has to safeguard what he has obtained because it is given freely.

Related Competencies:

- Assertiveness (too high)
- Interpersonal Relationships
- Empathy

45

You can succeed in life, no matter your circumstances, provided you have determination and follow the path of the superior person.

The superior person perseveres no matter what. He has confidence in himself and the assertiveness to step up and do what needs to be done. He knows what he values and cultivates a lifestyle that reflects those values. This leads to success. How many people fail because they give up too quickly? See it through to completion no matter what.

Related Competencies:

- Self-Regard
- Self-Actualization
- Assertiveness

46

Through hardness and selfishness, the heart grows rigid, and this rigidity leads to separation from others.

The superior person shows compassion for others. He cultivates Empathy skills, Social Responsibility, and great relationships. He gives to others. He is flexible and engaged. This leads to success. People give you strength, encouragement, connections, opportunities, and ideas. When you are separated from others, you lose those opportunities, and that will lead to failure.

Related Competencies

- Interpersonal Relationships
- Empathy
- Social Responsibility
- Flexibility

47

Slander will be silenced if we do not gratify it with injured retorts.

Our first reaction to slander is to defend, justify, show people the "truth". But the superior person does not reply. He knows that any reply only prolongs the discussion at hand. By not responding, he is showing his superior nature, his self-confidence, and the slanderer will be silenced.

Related Competencies:

- Self-Regard
- Emotional Expression (too high)
- Impulse Control

48

In friendships and close relationships, you must make a careful choice.

Some people fill you up. Others drain you. The superior person knows that the drainers only take things away from him. So he tries to surround himself with fillers. Those positive people tend to congregate and feed off each other's energy. Choose carefully those who are close to you. Find those people who lift you up and support you.

Related Competencies:

- Interpersonal Relationships
- Reality Testing

49

Power best expresses itself in gentleness.

The inferior person bullies and uses his power in a negative way. The people underneath him are resentful and are always plotting to overthrow or undermine him. The superior person is naturally gentle in nature. People feel safe with him and know that he will never do them harm. They will support him and honor him.

Related Competencies:

- Emotional Expression
- Assertiveness (too high)
- Interpersonal Relationships
- Empathy
- Social Responsibility

50

In exercises in meditation and concentration, trying to force results will lead to an unwholesome outcome.

Water has a calm approach, but can wear away the largest rock by slow and steady force. The superior person acts like water, composing himself internally and having a calm, steady approach. This will lead to success and the desired outcome.

Related Competencies:

- Self-Actualization
- Assertiveness
- Impulse Control
- Stress Tolerance

51

Do not complain. Enjoy the good fortune you still possess.

When faced with adversity, the inferior person complains. He whines and moans about his unfortunate circumstances and blames others for it. The superior person counts his blessings and knows that his blessings far outweigh his bad fortune. He is generally happy in all circumstances. He responds to negative events in a positive way, thus ensuring a positive outcome for the future.

Related Competencies:

- Self-Actualization
- Emotional Expression (too high)
- Stress Tolerance
- Optimism
- Happiness

52

For power to be truly great it must remain inwardly united with the fundamental principles of right and justice.

The superior person always has a touchstone of principles to rely on. He is grounded in these principles. Truly great men don't forget this once they have attained power. The inferior person is corrupted by power and forgets his principles.

Related Competencies:

- Self-Actualization
- Social Responsibility

53

Not a whole day.

When the superior person sees that something needs doing, that something needs correcting, that something needs his attention, he will not let a day pass before taking action.

Related Competencies:

- Assertiveness
- Problem Solving

54

The way of the superior person is to be joyous in heart, yet concerned in thought.

The superior person knows to prepare for the future and that people will let him down. He is concerned with these thoughts, but does not let it ruin his present happiness. He lives in the present with joy and looks forward to the future with cautious Optimism.

Related Competencies:

- Emotional Self-Awareness
- Reality Testing
- Stress Tolerance
- Optimism
- Happiness

55

The superior person is completely sincere in his thoughts and actions.

People can spot phonies a mile away. The superior person cultivates sincerity in all of his thoughts and actions. And if he cannot be sincere, he does not try to manufacture feelings. He tries to be honest with his thoughts and feelings. The superior person is simple in his approach and makes connections with others on a very basic, human level. At first, this may not come easy to some. But if you continue on this path of the superior person, this sincerity will be cultivated so that no matter what situation you are in, you will act with a sincere heart and mind.

Related Competencies:

- Emotional Self-Awareness
- Emotional Expression
- Interpersonal Relationships
- Reality Testing

56

Those things in our psychic body later manifest in our physical body.

The more we study modern medicine, the more we see the mind/ body connection. The superior person cultivates a healthy approach mentally, physically, spiritually, and emotionally. The whole theory is that what our minds think, we manifest. We are energy, and when we vibrate at different frequencies, we get different results. Pay attention to what you are thinking. If you are thinking predominantly negative thoughts, this will lead to failure, illness, and negative results.

Related Competencies:

- Stress Tolerance
- Optimism
- Happiness

57

At the beginning of a project, if many boastful claims are made, the successful attainment of the goal becomes far more difficult.

The superior person will be modest in his assessment of a project's outcome. He will keep his ego in check and prepare the stakeholders for potential problems that may arise. This will instill confidence and ensure that stakeholders will not be disappointed.

Related Competencies:

- Self-Regard (too high)
- Emotional Expression
- Problem Solving
- Reality Testing
- Optimism (too high)

58

Even small power, used correctly, can achieve great success.

The superior person creates a goal, fixes his mind upon it, and plans accordingly to achieve success. Don't cry about what you don't have, but use what you do have to your greatest advantage.

Related Competencies:

- Assertiveness
- Problem Solving

59

If you would rule, first learn to serve.

There is much talk about servant leadership. The superior person puts himself into the shoes of the people he will be over. He understands their needs and their motivations and cultivates relationships with them. The inferior person uses his authority without regard to the ones he has authority over. This creates resentment and resistance and will lead to failure.

Related Competencies:

- Interpersonal Relationships
- Empathy
- Social Responsibility

60

Do not allow yourself to be led astray by a leader.

Be a good follower, but never allow a leader to compromise your integrity. When you see them doing something wrong, you should point it out and you should never give into them just because they are in a higher position.

Related Competencies:

- Independence

61

Through words and deeds the superior person moves heaven and earth.

The superior person knows that his words and deeds create success or failure. He is vigilant about what he says and does and uses his Impulse Control to avoid false steps. These good things come from deep within and are tied to his values and principles.

Related Competencies:

- Self-Actualization
- Emotional Expression
- Impulse Control

62

If one clings to the little boy, one loses the strong man.

The superior person knows when to leave childish ways of thinking behind. You must become a strong, independent person to be successful and to be fully actualized.

Related Competencies:

- Self-Actualization
- Independence
- Reality Testing

63

Take not gain or loss to heart. What man holds high comes to nothing.

Do not gage your worth by your gain. They are separate things. Anything you have gained or lost are no longer valid when you die. So don't dwell on gains or losses. Stay in the moment and live.

Related Competencies:

- Self-Actualization
- Optimism
- Happiness

64

You have received a nature that is innately good. When your thoughts and actions are in accord with your nature, you will enjoy great good fortune and supreme success.

The inferior person gives into base things such as greed, selfishness, cruelty, and hatred. This draws all things negative to him. The superior person cultivates feelings of love, compassion, joy, and selflessness. He experiences Happiness. You experience what you intend.

Related Competencies:

- Self-Actualization
- Optimism
- Happiness

65

To remain at the mercy of moods of hope and fear will cost you your inner composure and consistency.

If you are influenced by the hills and valleys of hope and despair, you will never achieve success. The superior person cultivates composure no matter what the circumstances. He lives a life filled with joy and certainty and courage. He knows that there is great power in this.

Related Competencies:

- Self-Actualization
- Happiness

66

To be a superior person, see to it that goodness is an established attribute of character rather than an accidental and isolated occurrence.

The superior person always tries to benefit others. His intentions are always good. This takes diligence and Emotional Self-Awareness as we have a tendency to go down those bad roads, especially under times of stress.

Related Competencies:

- Self-Regard
- Self-Actualization
- Emotional Self-Awareness

67

Conflict within weakens the power to conquer danger without.

The superior person is sure in his beliefs and values and acts upon them without hesitation. Conflict on a team will prevent the team from acting appropriately. The inferior person hesitates because he is not sure how to proceed. He has no foundation to work from.

Related Competencies:

- Self-Regard
- Self-Actualization
- Emotional Self-Awareness
- Assertiveness
- Independence
- Social Responsibility
- Impulse Control

68

Don't be ashamed of simplicity or small means.

The superior person strives for simplicity because he knows it is a real strength. The inferior person has no confidence and is ostentatious in his approach. Keep it simple.

Related Competencies:

- Self-Regard
- Self-Actualization

69

If you are not as you should be, you will have misfortune, and it does not further you to undertake anything.

The inferior person usually makes his own misery, and he does not see that he causes most of his own problems. The superior person knows he has strength of character and will be able to undertake anything and be successful.

Related Competencies:

- Emotional Self-Awareness
- Problem Solving
- Happiness

70

Danger has an important and beneficial use.

When you see danger, you take the necessary precautions, you plan and are aware of what might happen.

Related Competencies:

- Reality Testing
- Optimism (too high)

71

Words are movements going from within, outward. Eating and drinking are movements that go from without, inward. Both movements can be modified by tranquility.

The superior person cultivates calm and peace and centeredness. He is always composed and mindful of everything he does. He is always in the moment and aware of his actions and their consequences. He is fully present. Therefore, whether he is speaking, eating, or drinking, he does so in moderation.

Related Competencies:

- Emotional Self-Awareness
- Emotional Expression
- Impulse Control
- Stress Tolerance

72

Passion and reason cannot exist side by side.

When you experience strong emotions, you cannot think clearly. When those emotions arise, the superior person calms himself before acting.

Related Competencies:

- Emotional Self-Awareness
- Emotional Expression
- Assertiveness
- Reality Testing
- Impulse Control

73

Exceptional enterprises cannot succeed unless the utmost caution is observed in their beginnings.

The superior person pays attention to all details prior to embarking on an endeavor. A small error in the beginning grows as the project progresses. The superior person visualizes the outcome and takes the necessary steps to get him there.

Related Competencies:

- Emotional Self-Awareness
- Problem Solving

74

In the time of gathering together, make no arbitrary choice of your associates. There are secret forces at work, leading together those who belong together.

Have you had the feeling about someone that they just weren't right? The superior person listens to that voice within and chooses his companions accordingly. There are no accidental meetings. There is a purpose to everything and everyone you come into contact with. When choosing associates, be deliberate and use caution.

Related Competencies:

- Self-Actualization
- Emotional Self-Awareness
- Interpersonal Relationships
- Social Responsibility

75

In following the path of the superior person, slight digressions from the good cannot be avoided, but you must turn back before going too far.

We all get off track. Life gets in the way. That's why it is important to check in. Daily reflection is very beneficial. Check in with your development plan at least annually to see if there is anything that needs to be changed. Build in measurement and accountability so that you will know when you are getting off track and take the steps to get back on.

Related Competencies:

- Self-Actualization
- Impulse Control
- Flexibility
- Stress Tolerance

76

In the hands of a great master, all material is productive.

The superior person finds a use for everything and everybody. Since there is nothing wasted, he always has what he needs. He sees value in everyone. He cultivates great relationships. He utilizes everything within his reach and creates great value.

Related Competencies:

- Self-Actualization
- Emotional Self-Awareness
- Interpersonal Relationships
- Social Responsibility

77

Pleasant manners succeed even with irritable people.

If you go into a situation thinking about a good outcome, it will affect the outcome. The opposite is also true. If you go in expecting the worst, then that's what you will probably get. Don't react to irritable people, but hold an optimistic viewpoint at all times.

Related Competencies:

- Emotional Self-Awareness
- Emotional Expression
- Interpersonal Relationships
- Empathy
- Impulse Control
- Optimism

78

To enjoy a meaningful way of life, and to produce long lasting effects, the ability to endure must be firmly established within you.

The superior person perseveres through all adversity and obstacles. It is firmly embedded in his character and in his life plan. He has the confidence to carry him through anything and the Assertiveness to make things happen.

Related Competencies:

- Self-Regard
- Self-Actualization
- Assertiveness

79

The superior person sees and understands the transitory in the light of eternity.

The superior person stays in the moment because that is all that there is. Life is so fleeting, and the superior person makes every moment count. He does not waste his life on frivolous pursuits.

Related Competencies:

- Self-Actualization
- Impulse Control
- Stress Tolerance

80

Mad pursuit of pleasure never takes one to the goal.

The superior person doesn't give in to base desires, but keeps his eyes on his values and principles as laid out in his life plan. This leads to great success and Happiness.

Related Competencies:

- Self-Actualization
- Impulse Control
- Happiness

81

Every person must have something to follow: a lodestar.

Everyone needs direction and a life plan. That way, when you get off track, you can always refer to it.

Related Competencies:

- Self-Actualization

82

Every ending contains a new beginning.

Successful people do one thing that unsuccessful people don't do. They take action. If you are on the path of the inferior person, you only have to end that journey and begin to take the path of the superior person. Take action today. Don't put it off.

Related Competencies:

•   Self-Actualization

I-CHING Table

Find the competencies that you are going to improve. If you see an "h" by the number listed, it means that if this competency is too high, it can be problematic.

Read the associated I Ching saying each day and make that saying the focus for your day. Remember to apply the sayings in the context of improving the emotional competence.

You may also download our app, The Tao of Emotional Intelligence. It will automatically choose a saying for you based on the competency you have chosen.

Self Perception Composite	
Self-Regard	2h 3h 10h 18 19 24 25h 26 27 30 32h 39 41 45 47 57h 66 67 68 78
Self-Actualization	4 7 9 11 12 15 19 24 26 27 28 33 34 35 36 38 43 45 51 52 61 62 63 64 65 66 67 68 74 75 76 78 79 80 81 82
Emotional Self-Awareness	1 2 3 4 7 11 13 15 18 19 20 21 24 25 30 33 34 39 40 54 55 66 67 69 71 72 73 74 76 77
Self Expression Composite	
Emotional Expression	5 17 25 29 31 32 37 42 47h 49 51h 55 57h 61 71 72 77
Assertiveness	5 13 17 19 21h 29 35 44h 45 49h 50 53 58 67 72 78
Independence	13 16 18 30 41 60 62
Interpersonal Composite	
Interpersonal Relationships	4 11 13 21 22 23 25 27 28 32 37 44 46 48 49 55 59 74 76 77
Empathy	4 13 16 19 21 25 29 37 39 44 46 49 59 77
Social Responsibility	13 21 22 25 46 49 52 59 67 74 76
Decision Making Composite	
Problem Solving	1 2 3 4 5 6 8 10 12 17 18 19 20 21 23 24 35 37 43 53 57 58 69 73

Reality Testing	1 2 4 8 9 10 12 15 16 20 21 23 24 27 35 37 38 43 48 54 55 57 62 70 72
Impulse Control	5 6 7 8 9 11 12 14 15 16 19 20 21 29 30 34 37 39 40 42 43 47 50 61 67 71 72 75 77 79 80
Stress Management Composite	
Flexibility	1 8 7h 10 12h 13h 21 23 37 42h 43 46 75
Stress Tolerance	6 12 14 18 19 33 34 36 40 50 51 54 56 71 75 79
Optimism	2h 8 10h 17 20h 26 28 31 34 36 51 54 56 57h 63 64 70h 77
Well Being Indicator	
Happiness	1 7 9 11 12 14 15 26 28 29 31 33 34 51 54 56 63 64 65 69 80